RESCUE ME

ISBN 979-8-88644-678-4 (Paperback)
ISBN 979-8-88644-679-1 (Digital)

Covenant Books
11661 Hwy 707
Murrells Inlet, SC 29576
www.covenantbooks.com

RESCUE ME

A Story about Bella and Jax Rescue Dogs

Heather Virgulto

A tan six-month-old dog at a pet rescue center says, "I want to find a home, I want to be loved." She was a pretty and stubborn dog. She is tan and has a little bit of black and white on her body and face. She wanted a home. She wanted to be loved.

Somewhere else, in another shelter, a dog thinks, "I want to find a family who loves me and plays with me. I am so handsome with nice black, soft, and shiny fur."

The tan dog that was at the pet store thinks, "Hopefully, someone will find me to love." The black dog also hoped someone would come and find him a home. He wanted to play.

At the pet store adoption, many dogs did not have a home.
They wanted someone to love and care for them.

They did not like being in cages and wanted a place to call
home.

On this day, the tan dog saw a girl, and she wagged her tail in delight. The girl liked this dog and decided to take her out of her cage.

Well, both the girl Emily and the dog got along just fine. The tan dog lay on her lap and seemed so happy.

Emily liked her so much that she decided to adopt her and named her Bella.

On a different day, a man went to see the black dog, a six-month-old black lab; he was so shy and scared.

The man knew he needed to help him. He thought of the tan dog Bella. He thought about how she was rescued, so maybe they would be good together.

The man brought his new dog *Jax*, which he named, to see Bella, the tan dog.

They saw each other, sniffed each other, and ran around and played.

They found each other, they were rescued, and they found a family.

They have been together ever since, side by side, to take on many adventures together!

Rescue a dog from a shelter or agency. They need a home and love. More stories about *Bella and Jax Adventures* continue. Look out for the new book coming soon. Bella and Jax have a family, and Bella and Jax go camping.

ABOUT THE AUTHOR

Heather Virgulto was born in Connecticut. She did not have many animals growing up. After buying a full-bred German shepherd and having to put it down by two years old, she was saddened by the process of full-bred dogs. Sometimes inhumane conditions they are born into. Once she was on her own and adopted a rescue dog, her life changed. The love and dedication of her rescue dog brought her unconditional love. One she never experienced with an animal. Her pop always told her she was a good writer. After adopting now three rescue dogs and seeing how loving and caring they can be, she decided to bring light to the adoption process of these needy animals. Heather was inspired by the two dogs that have been rescued and have lived a good life and gave it back twofold. Loving and caring for dogs in need have inspired her to write this book and the words of her pop. Pets have so much love to give, and she wants to bring more attention to rescuing dogs or animals that need a home and people to love.